A3 Problem-Solving Made Simple for Beginners:

Start Solving, Start Succeeding!

Dear Reader,

Thank you for embarking on this journey of learning and growth with us. Your dedication to exploring the principles of problem-solving and continuous improvement is truly inspiring.

As you close this book, remember that every challenge is an opportunity for growth, and every setback is a chance to innovate. Stay curious, stay determined, and never underestimate the power of your ideas.

Let's continue to strive for excellence, push boundaries, and make a positive impact in all that we do.

With gratitude,

VitalBooks

Table of Contents

Introduction to A3 Problem Solving – (Page 5)

Part I: The Start (Page 10)

Understanding the Problem and Finding the Root Cause

- Defining the Problem Statement
- Identifying the Scope of the Problem
- Gathering Data and Facts
- Root Cause Analysis

Part II: The Plan (Page 43)

Developing Countermeasures and Action Plans

- Brainstorming sessions
- Benchmarking
- Pilot Programs
- Evaluating and Prioritizing Solutions
- Creating Your Action Plans

Part III: Mastering A3 Methodology (Page 63)

Structuring, Implementing, and Follow-up

- The A3 Report
- Tips for Effective Communication
- Implementation and Follow-up

Part IV: Extras (Page 77)

- Case Studies
- Continuous Improvement
- and More

Conclusion – (Page 100)

Introduction to A3 Problem Solving

Imagine being lost in a maze without a map. Each twist and turn presents a new obstacle, and without a clear path forward, you're left wandering aimlessly. This is the reality of many problems we encounter in both our personal and professional lives—complex, daunting, and seemingly insurmountable. A3 problem-solving offers us that much-needed map, providing a systematic approach to navigate through the intricacies of our challenges.

In today's fast-paced environment, organizations and professionals alike face a myriad of challenges that demand effective problem-solving skills. Whether you're an entrepreneur that's navigating the complexities of a startup, a corporate leader seeking to drive continuous improvement, or an individual striving for personal growth, the ability to identify and resolve problems systematically can be a game-changer. A3 problem solving is a structured and systematic approach to problem-solving that originated from the Toyota Production System (TPS) and has since been adopted by numerous highly successful organizations worldwide.

Enter the A3 Problem-Solving methodology – a structured approach that empowers you to tackle challenges head-on, uncover root causes, and implement sustainable solutions. Rooted in the principles of lean management and continuous improvement, the A3 model offers a practical framework that condenses complex problems onto a single sheet of paper, fostering clarity, collaboration, and actionable insights. The term "A3" refers to the standard paper size—11 inches by 17 inches (or A3 in metric)—used to document the problem-solving process. A3 problem solving is more than just a tool; it's a mindset that encourages continuous improvement and empowers individuals at all levels of an organization to identify and solve problems effectively.

Now, you might be wondering how A3 problem-solving can benefit you—whether you're tackling workplace challenges, business solutions, or navigating the complexities of everyday life. Without a structured approach, you will find yourself spinning your wheels, trying one solution after another with little success because your problem-solving strategy has no dependable foundation. But with A3 problem-solving in your toolkit, you're equipped with a systematic method to break down the problem, identify its root causes, and develop targeted solutions. Suddenly, what once seemed unconquerable becomes manageable, and you're empowered to drive meaningful change.

The beauty of this book lies in its ability to serve as your comprehensive guide to mastering the A3 problem-solving methodology, regardless of your current level of expertise. With a wealth of practical examples, step-by-step instructions, and real-world case studies, it offers a roadmap for applying this powerful tool effectively within your organization or personal endeavors. By delving into the nuances of A3 problem-solving, you'll not only drive innovation and efficiency but also lay the foundation for sustainable success in tackling complex challenges.

Why A3 Problem Solving is Important

The importance of A3 problem-solving lies not only in its ability to guide us through the problem-solving process but also in its emphasis on clarity and transparency. By condensing our thoughts, analyses, and solutions onto a single sheet of paper or document, we're forced to distill complex ideas into their most essential components.

This not only fosters a deeper understanding of the problem personally, but also facilitates effective communication and collaboration among team members. At its core, A3 problem solving provides a framework for tackling problems in a methodical manner, leading to more efficient and effective outcomes. Without structure, problem-solving is a means to never finding an end.

By using a structured approach, you can:

Identify Root Causes - A3 problem solving emphasizes the importance of digging deep to uncover the underlying causes of problems rather than merely addressing symptoms. By understanding the root causes, organizations can implement targeted solutions that address the core issues, leading to long-lasting improvements.

Promote Collaboration and Communication - The A3 process encourages cross-functional collaboration and communication by involving key participants from different departments or teams. By bringing diverse perspectives together, organizations can leverage collective wisdom to develop innovative solutions and foster a culture of teamwork.

Drive Continuous Improvement - A3 problem solving is not a one-time fix but rather a continuous improvement methodology. By incorporating A3 problem solving continuously, organizations can iterate on solutions, monitor results, and adjust as necessary to achieve ongoing improvement.

In essence, A3 problem-solving is more than just a methodology—it's a mindset. It encourages us to approach problems with clarity, curiosity, and creativity. By embracing this approach, we not only become more effective problem solvers but also catalysts for positive change in our own lives and the world around us. So, as we embark on this journey together, let us embrace the power of A3 problem-solving to unlock new possibilities and chart a course towards a brighter future.

In today's competitive landscape, organizations and individuals that embrace A3 problem solving gain a competitive edge by becoming more agile, responsive, and adaptive to change. Whether you're streamlining processes, improving efficiency, reducing expenses, or enhancing company culture, the principles of A3 problem solving can be applied to a wide range of challenges, making it a valuable tool for organizations and individuals alike.

In the upcoming chapters, we'll dive into the core components of the A3 problem-solving process, dissecting each aspect comprehensively and offering actionable insights alongside real-world examples. By breaking down the intricacies of each step, we aim to equip you with practical tools and knowledge to navigate this methodology with confidence. Our goal is to provide a straightforward and accessible approach to problem-solving, tailored for individuals at any expertise level or professional background. Whether you're a seasoned professional or just starting your journey, this book will empower you to tackle challenges effectively and drive meaningful change in your organization or personal endeavors.

With that being said, let's embark on this journey together and unlock the potential for transformative change through A3 problem-solving!

Part I: The Start

Understanding the Problem

and Finding the Root Cause

A problem well stated is a problem half solved.

--John Dewey

The Start

In the realm of problem-solving, the initial phase is vital: understanding the problem in its entirety. However, before we can effectively address these issues, it is crucial to have a clear understanding of the problem at hand. The first step in effective problem-solving is developing a deep understanding of the problem and its identity. This section will guide you through the maze of understanding the problem using three proven techniques.

Part I delves into three main factors of understanding the problem which includes:

1. Defining the Problem Statement
2. Identifying the Scope of the Problem
3. Gathering Data and Facts

By defining the problem statement, identifying its scope, and gathering relevant data and facts, you can take the first fundamental steps in the process.

Think as if you are a homebuilder who is about to build a house. Before laying the foundation or hammering the first nail, you need a clear blueprint outlining the design, dimensions, and materials required. Similarly, defining the problem statement, identifying its scope, and gathering relevant data and facts serve as the blueprint for problem-solving. Just as a well-crafted blueprint ensures the construction proceeds smoothly and efficiently, these initial steps provide the groundwork necessary to navigate the problem-solving process effectively. They help set the parameters, establish goals, and provide a solid foundation upon which to build viable solutions.

Whether you're facing organizational challenges or personal dilemmas, delving into these initial steps lays the groundwork for a thorough understanding of the problem. This understanding serves as the compass guiding you towards viable solutions.

Defining the Problem Statement

Imagine setting sail on a vast ocean with the destination obscured by fog. Without a clear understanding of your course, navigating becomes challenging and uncertain. Similarly, in problem-solving, defining the problem acts as the compass guiding our journey towards a solution. It illuminates the issue at hand, reveals its impact, and clarifies its significance and objectives. Once the problem is defined, we can chart the scope of our exploration, setting the course for effective problem-solving.

Defining the problem statement should answer three pivotal questions:

What is the problem? – Articulating the issue at hand.

Who is affected by it? – Describe its impact.

Why is it important? – Its significance and overall objective.

Without a well-defined definition to a problem, efforts to solve the problem may be misdirected, leading to wasted time and resources. For example, let's consider a shoe manufacturing company experiencing a decline in product quality, leading to a decline in sales and customer satisfaction.

The problem at first can be defined as:

"The manufacturing process is yielding an increasing number of defective products, leading to customer complaints and reduced profitability."

However, although that statement is factual for the company, it doesn't expose the potential culprit of where the problem is stemming from. So, let's break down the shoe manufacturing companies' problem statement and redefine it using our three pivotal questions stated above. These questions should serve as the starting point in understanding the problem in detail, allowing you to figure out the potential culprit of the problem.

What is the problem? - Articulating the problem at hand

In the context of our shoe manufacturing company, the problem lies in the increasing number of defective products detected during the final inspection stage of the manufacturing process. Upon closer examination, it becomes evident that these defects are primarily occurring in the stitching phase within the factories, where seams are not meeting quality standards.

Therefore, after digging deeper into the issue, the problem for the company statement could be reframed as:

"*The problem we are addressing is the rise in defective shoes due to stitching errors during the final inspection stage of the manufacturing process, leading to customer complaints and reduced profitability.*"

Who is affected by it? - Describe its impact

The impact of these defects ripples within and beyond the organization. Just as persistent car troubles cause inconvenience and expenses for car owners, the defective shoes result in dissatisfaction among customers and a negative impact on the financial wellbeing of the company. Moreover, the company's reputation and credibility in the shoe market are at risk, as customers expect high-quality products. Internally, the cost of rework, returns, and potential loss of future business due to poor quality stitching significantly impacts the company's bottom line, affecting employees and shareholders alike.

Why is it important to address? - Its significance and overall objective

Understanding the significance and overall objective of the problem is crucial for guiding the shoe company manufacturers' efforts towards positive improvement. By recognizing the significance of defective products on customer satisfaction, profitability, and reputation, the company can prioritize its objectives effectively moving forward. In this case, after realizing the significance of the stitching defects, the main goal of the company would be trying to define the key objectives that will enhance product quality and customer satisfaction while improving profitability.

An example of a potential objective after realizing the problems' significance would be to reduce the number of defective products by 30% within the next six months allowing the company to improve customer satisfaction and increase profitability. This objective encompasses the specific goals of reducing stitching defects, increasing customer loyalty, and optimizing operational efficiency. By focusing on the significance of the problem and the objective(s) that can resolve the issue, the shoe company can effectively align its efforts with the needs of its customers and work towards continuing sustainable growth and success.

By applying these questions to the shoe manufacturing company, we can see how they help articulate the problem, describe who's affected, and define its significance and necessary objectives that ultimately guide the company to an effective strategy to fix the issue. This structured approach not only ensures that the main questions to the problem are answered, but also leads to the next step in the A3 process, which is identifying the scope of the problem.

Identifying the Scope of the Problem

Once we've articulated the problem statement, the next crucial step is to define the scope of the problem. In simpler terms, identifying the scope of the problem is a fancy way of pinpointing what exactly is causing the problem in the first place. This involves defining the specific factor(s) causing the problem, understanding the boundaries and limitations of the issue, as well as identifying any related factors that may influence or contribute to it.

Understanding the scope is essential because it prevents us from attempting to solve a problem that is either too broad or too narrow. It allows us to focus our efforts on specific areas where we can have the most significant impact and avoid getting overwhelmed by irrelevant details that may steer us in the opposite direction. Let's delve deeper into the scope of the problem using our shoe manufacturing company and use other examples to further emphasize how to identify the scope.

Defining Boundaries: Defining the boundaries involves identifying the specific parameters within each problem and determining what can be included and excluded from consideration during the problem-solving process. For the shoe manufacturing company, defining the boundaries of the problem entails specifying the areas of focus within the production process that can correct the stitching issue.

For instance, the scope after defining boundaries would be:

"Our problem encompasses the stitching phase of the manufacturing process, where defects are identified during the final inspection before products reach customers. We will concentrate on factors such as stitching techniques, machinery calibration, and quality control procedures."

This defines the specific factors that can be contributing to their defective products and targets the specific processes that produce the stitching on the shoes. Defining boundaries within the scope of a problem allows you to narrow the focus down to the processes, systems, or other factors that are more than likely causing the actual problem.

Considering Interdependencies: Defining the scope of the problem is just one step. You also have to consider any factors that may be the direct influence behind the issue. Interdependencies describe the connections between different factors or elements that affect a particular situation or problem. It's about understanding how various parts of a system or process interact with each other and how changes in one aspect can impact others and create other potential issues. In essence, it's recognizing what is interconnected and that addressing one issue may involve considering its effects on other related aspects as well. This allows all the moving parts within the problem to be placed under a family tree, providing you with a crystal-clear blueprint of the bigger picture and a precise pathway to eventually finding the main influence of the problem.

For the shoe manufacturing company, they also have interconnected factors influencing product quality. For example, factors such as the quality of raw materials, the reliability of suppliers, and the skill level of production workers can all contribute to the occurrence of stitching defects. Therefore, the company must also evaluate all the interconnected factors within the shoe making process to figure out if any of those variables can be the cause of the stitching defects also.

Overall, considering interdependencies allows us to take a more comprehensive approach to problem-solving, addressing not only the immediate symptoms but also the underlying causes that can potentially contribute to the problem as well. Recognizing these interdependencies is crucial for identifying root causes and implementing effective solutions.

Clarifying Constraints: Clarifying constraints consists of identifying the limitations that can restrict our actions or solutions when addressing a problem that needs to be solved. It involves understanding specific rules, regulations, resources, or other factors that we must work within or around to find effective solutions. In general, clarifying constraints is about recognizing the boundaries of what is possible or permissible in addressing the problem at hand and what potential hoops and hurdles one must go through to achieve the end goal.

For our shoe manufacturing company, compliance with quality standards and safety regulations within the industry imposes constraints on the production process. Additionally, budget constraints may limit investments in technology upgrades or employee training programs aimed at improving product quality. By clarifying these constraints, our shoe manufacturing company can develop strategies and action plans that consider the specific limitations and challenges it potentially faces and how to overcome them.

This ensures that efforts to address the problem of increasing defective products are realistic, achievable, and aligned with the company's overall goals and constraints.

Overall, clarifying constraints is about understanding the potential limitations that impact our decisions and actions. By identifying these constraints early on, we can anticipate challenges, plan accordingly, and develop strategies that take into account the specific boundaries within which we must operate. This proactive approach allows us to address obstacles more effectively and increases the likelihood of success in solving problems or reaching our objectives.

Now, let's go over a few other examples using different industries to further elaborate on how to effectively identify the scope of the problem.

Entrepreneurial Ventures

Defining Boundaries: Suppose an entrepreneurial venture, such as a software startup, is struggling with user retention. In this case, the scope could be defined as focusing on the onboarding process, user engagement strategies, and product feature enhancements to address the problem effectively.

Considering Interdependencies: While the startup is struggling with user retention, interdependencies might include product functionality, customer support responsiveness, and marketing effectiveness. Addressing these interdependencies collectively can also lead to improved user engagement and retention rates.

Clarifying Restraints: Regulatory compliance with data protection laws and financial constraints may limit the scope of product development and marketing efforts for a software startup. By understanding these constraints, entrepreneurs can prioritize initiatives that align with regulatory requirements and available resources.

Retail Management

Defining Boundaries: In a retail store facing declining sales, the scope might involve evaluating the store layout, merchandising strategies, and customer service practices. For instance, the scope can be defined as focusing on the checkout process efficiency, product placement, and staff training to improve overall sales performance.

Considering Interdependencies: In a retail store facing declining sales, interdependencies could involve factors such as inventory management, pricing strategies, and customer satisfaction levels. By understanding how these factors interact, retailers can develop comprehensive solutions to boost sales performance and enhance the overall shopping experience.

Clarifying Constraints: Budget limitations may restrict investments in store renovations or technology upgrades aimed at enhancing the customer experience in the store. Understanding these constraints allows retailers to identify cost-effective strategies for improving sales performance while staying within budgetary constraints.

Project Management

Defining Boundaries: For a construction project experiencing delays, the scope could be defined as focusing on specific phases of the project, such as site preparation, material procurement, and construction scheduling. This approach allows project managers to identify critical issues and streamline processes to mitigate delays effectively.

Considering Interdependencies: For a construction project experiencing delays, interdependencies might encompass factors like weather conditions, material availability, and subcontractor scheduling. Recognizing these interdependencies allows project managers to anticipate potential challenges and implement proactive measures to mitigate risks and minimize project delays.

Clarifying Constraints: Regulatory approvals and budget constraints may impact the timeline and resources allocated to construction projects. By clarifying these constraints upfront, project managers can develop realistic project plans and allocate resources efficiently to ensure project success within regulatory and budgetary constraints.

Gathering Data and Facts

Gathering data and facts comes next after identifying the scope of the problem. Once you have defined the problem and clarified the boundaries and limitations of the problem, the next step is to collect relevant information that will help you understand the problem more deeply to identify any potential causes or contributing factors in more detail.

To make informed decisions and develop effective solutions, it is essential to gather relevant information and objective facts related to the problem. Data provides the necessary evidence needed to understand the root causes of the problem and evaluate the effectiveness of potential solutions. Without data or hard facts, our decisions and strategies can become irrelevant to solving the problem.

Identifying Relevant Data Sources: Identifying relevant data sources is crucial as it ensures that the information collected is directly related to the problem at hand. This step involves determining where to find the necessary data to gain insights into the problem and potential solutions. This ties into the premise of gathering facts and data to identify the sources that directly relate to the problem or situation.

For example, in a shoe manufacturing company experiencing stitching defects, relevant data sources may include production logs, quality control reports, and employee feedback. For entrepreneurs and professionals, this involves determining where to find the necessary information to address challenges or capitalize on opportunities. For instance, an entrepreneur looking to understand customer preferences might gather data from market research, customer feedback, and competitor analysis.

Similarly, a project manager seeking to improve team performance may collect data from employee surveys, project reports, and performance evaluations. By identifying the data sources directly related to the problem, you can access valuable insights to guide your strategies and actions effectively.

By pinpointing data sources that relate directly to the problem, you can gather accurate and comprehensive data to positively influence decision-making and address the root cause(s) of the problem. Data serves as a guide in problem-solving efforts, helping us make informed decisions, create effective strategies, and find sustainable solutions to every problem that comes our way.

Here are powerful ways to gather data and facts:

Quantitative Data Collection: Quantitative data collection involves gathering numerical information to analyze trends and patterns. For the shoe manufacturing company, this could mean examining production logs to track defect rates over time or studying maintenance records to identify equipment malfunctions affecting productivity. For instance, by analyzing production logs, the company may notice a consistent increase in defect rates after a specific machine was used to stitch the shoes, indicating the potential culprit of the problem.

Aside from larger organizations, entrepreneurs and professionals can gather quantitative data through various methods such as market research, analyzing sales and financial records, and monitoring website analytics. For example, an entrepreneur launching a new product might conduct market research surveys to collect numerical data on customer preferences and purchasing behavior. Similarly, a marketing manager for a company might analyze website traffic data to track the effectiveness of online campaigns and optimize marketing strategies based on quantitative metrics like conversion rates and click-through rates.

Qualitative Data Collection: Qualitative data collection involves gathering descriptive information through methods such as interviews or factual observations. In the context of our shoe manufacturer, this could entail interviewing employees to gain insights into workflow challenges or observing production processes first-hand to identify inefficiencies in the shoe stitching process. For instance, conducting interviews with experienced workers may reveal communication breakdowns between different departments contributing to stitching defects in the production line.

Entrepreneurs and professionals can gather qualitative data by conducting interviews, focus groups, and open-ended surveys. For example, a startup founder might conduct customer interviews to understand pain points and preferences regarding existing products or services to better service clients based on negative feedback received. Similarly, a human resources manager could organize focus groups to gather employee feedback on workplace culture and satisfaction based on frequent employee complaints to figure out how to improve employee satisfaction.

Qualitative data provides rich insights into attitudes, motivations, and perceptions, complementing quantitative data to offer a comprehensive understanding of the problem or situation at hand.

Analyzing Data: Once viable data is collected, it's important to analyze it to uncover patterns and insights. Analyzing data means looking closely at the information we've gathered to find patterns and useful insights. By doing this carefully, we can understand problems better and come up with good solutions. Analyzing data helps us figure out what's going on and decide what to do next.

For the shoe manufacturer, analyzing production data can reveal patterns in defect rates across various stages of manufacturing. By identifying correlations between variables such as equipment usage and defect occurrence based on data, the manufacturer can pinpoint areas for improvement and implement targeted solutions to reduce stitching defects and enhance product quality if those variables turn out to the actual cause of the problem.

Similarly, entrepreneurs and professionals can analyze data relevant to their respective fields to drive business success. For instance, an entrepreneur launching a new product line may analyze market research data to identify consumer preferences and market trends. By understanding customer behavior and demand, they can tailor their products or marketing strategies to meet market needs effectively to increase their chances of success. Professionals in project management might analyze project performance data to identify inefficiencies in workflows. By examining metrics such as project timelines, resource utilization, and team productivity, they can optimize processes and improve project outcomes more effectively.

In short, while gathering data and facts might seem overwhelming at first, it's like a flashlight in the dark - it helps us see things more clearly and make smarter decisions. Therefore, don't be afraid to dive into the numbers and information you can find while implementing the A3 methodology. Whether you're sourcing data alone or seeking outside help to gather data, it can serve as your ally in solving problems and achieving success. It sets the stage for subsequent steps, facilitating informed decisions and sustainable solutions that address the root causes of the problem in full confidence.

Root Cause Analysis

Root Cause Analysis is a vital tool in A3 problem-solving, especially when seeking to address recurring issues and improve their operations when defining the problem. It's also a great tool to use when the root cause isn't readily apparent at first, requiring you to delve into much deeper thought to find the main cause of the issue. At its core, root cause analysis aims to uncover the underlying causes of problems rather than merely addressing their symptoms. By identifying root causes, you can not only plan, but implement more effective and sustainable solutions in the long-term.

Root Cause Analysis can be seen as a detective tool for solving problems, especially for entities that want to fix things for good. Instead of just treating the surface issues, root cause analysis digs deep to find out what's really causing the problem. It's like pulling a weed from the ground, you must dig deep into the soil, grab it by its root, and pull it out so it doesn't grow back.

Tools for Root Cause Identification

Two highly effective tools for identifying root causes are the 5 Whys and the Fishbone Diagram, each bringing distinct advantages to the analysis process. These tools are not only valuable for uncovering the root cause of new problems but also for addressing any unexpected issues that may arise. They offer a systematic approach to dissecting problems comprehensively, providing highly valuable insights into the underlying factors driving the issue. Let's delve deeper into each tool and explore how they can aid organizations and individuals in pinpointing the root cause.

The 5 Whys

The 5 Whys technique is a straightforward yet powerful method for uncovering root causes by asking a series of "why" questions. The premise of the 5 Whys technique is to identify the root cause of a problem by asking "why" repeatedly to uncover deeper layers of the problem.

The name "5 Whys" suggests that asking "why" five times is often sufficient to reach the underlying cause of an issue. However, there can be more or fewer than five "whys" depending on the complexity of the problem and the depth of analysis required. The key is to continue asking "why" until reaching a point where further questioning does not yield meaningful insights or until identifying a clear and actionable root cause. It encourages deeper reflection and investigation into the factors behind a problem, helping to reveal underlying issues that may not be immediately apparent.

It's also essential to apply critical thinking and avoid jumping to conclusions prematurely. Each "why" question should lead to a specific and actionable answer, ultimately guiding the identification of the root cause. However, there isn't a set list of specific why questions to ask. This tool requires proper brainstorming, thinking outside of the box, and thoughtful consideration.

Here are guidelines to follow with the *5 Whys* technique:

1. **Start with the Problem Statement:** Begin by clearly defining the problem statement. This serves as the starting point for the 5 Whys analysis and provides focus and direction to the process.

2. **Ask Open-Ended Questions:** Each "why" question should be open-ended and focused on probing deeper into the underlying factors contributing to the problem. Avoid leading questions or assumptions that may bias the investigation.

3. **Follow the Causal Chain:** As you ask successive "why" questions, follow the causal chain to trace back to the root cause of the problem. Each answer should lead

logically to the next question, revealing insights into the interconnected factors at play.

4. **Dig Deeper:** As you progress through the 5 Whys, delve even deeper into the underlying causes by exploring additional layers of the problem. Resist the temptation to accept surface-level explanations and continue asking "why" until you reach a point where further questioning does not yield meaningful insights.

5. **Use Data and Evidence:** Support your "whys" with data and evidence whenever possible. This helps validate your assumptions and ensures that conclusions are based on objective information rather than speculation.

6. **Involve Cross-Functional Bias:** Collaborate with others to gain diverse perspectives and insights into the problem. Different viewpoints of the situation can provide unique experiences and expertise that contribute to a comprehensive understanding of the root causes.

7. **Know When to Stop:** Determine when to stop the 5 Whys process based on the depth and complexity of the problem. Ideally, you should continue asking "why" until you reach a point where further questioning does not reveal new insights or when you identify a clear and actionable root cause.

8. **Focus on Actionable Insights:** Throughout the 5 Whys process, prioritize actionable insights that can inform decision-making and drive meaningful change to the overall situation directly.

The 5 Whys technique is a simple yet incredibly powerful tool for problem-solving. Each question will interconnect with the previous one, forming a causal chain that helps trace back to the root cause. It's like peeling an onion, where each layer represents a different aspect or contributing factor to the problem. By systematically digging deeper with each "why," we can uncover the underlying factors that lead to the issue, ultimately enabling us to address it at its core. By peeling back the layers, you can move beyond surface-level symptoms to identify the fundamental issues driving the problem.

Let's consider a retail company experiencing declining sales and how they would utilize the 5 whys as an example. Remember, implementing the 5 whys does not require a set of specific questions to ask. You must start with the problem statement first and work your way down by asking why until you have found the root cause of the problem.

Let's see how the retail store would use the 5 whys:

1. **Why are sales declining?** (First why)

    Because foot traffic has decreased. (First answer)

2. **Why has foot traffic decreased?** (Second why)

    Because competitors have launched aggressive marketing campaigns. (Second answer)

3. **Why haven't we responded to competitor campaigns effectively?** (Third why)

Because our marketing strategy lacks targeted messaging. (Third answer)

4. **Why does our marketing lack targeted messaging?** (Fourth why)

    Because we haven't conducted market research to understand customer preferences. (Fourth answer)

5. **Why haven't we conducted market research?** (Fifth why)

    Because it wasn't included in our budget allocation. (Fifth answer - Root Cause)

Now, let's go over another example of an entrepreneur who launched a new product but is struggling to generate sales:

1. **Why isn't the product selling?** (First why)

    Because online traffic to the product page is low. (First answer)

2. **Why is online traffic low?** (Second why)

    Because the product isn't appearing in search results. (Second answer)

3. **Why isn't the product appearing in search results?** (Third why)

    Because the product listing lacks relevant keywords and optimization. (Third answer)

4. **Why does the product listing lack optimization?** (Fourth why)

   Because the entrepreneur didn't conduct keyword research or optimize the listing. (Fourth answer)

5. **Why didn't the entrepreneur conduct keyword research?** (Fifth why)

   Because they underestimated the importance of search engine optimization (SEO) in product visibility. (Fifth answer - Root Cause)

By following these two examples and the guidelines above, teams and individuals can effectively navigate the 5 Whys process, uncovering root causes and driving continuous improvement in their problem-solving efforts. Although the process may seem tedious, carefully peeling the layers of the problem at hand will provide the clearest solutions during the process.

In essence, not only does the 5 Whys technique act as a powerhouse tool, it also:

- Encourages critical thinking by challenging assumptions and exploring causal relationships.

- Reveals underlying causes through successive iterations of "why" questions.

- Identifies systemic issues by tracing cause-and-effect relationships.

- Promotes healthier collaboration among cross-functional teams, fostering engagement and buy-in.
- Drives continuous improvement by fostering a culture of reflection, learning, and innovation.

Beyond the workplace, the principles of the 5 Whys can be applied to various real-life situations, from personal relationships to everyday challenges. Whether diagnosing the root cause of a recurring issue in a household appliance or understanding the underlying motivations behind a behavioral pattern, the 5 Whys can help individuals gain clarity and take effective action.

In summary, the 5 Whys technique is a valuable tool for problem-solving, offering a structured approach to uncovering root causes and driving meaningful change. By embracing the process of asking "why," organizations and individuals alike can navigate complexities, overcome obstacles, and achieve sustainable success.

Fishbone Diagram

The Fishbone Diagram, also known as the Ishikawa or Cause-and-Effect Diagram, provides a structured way to visualize the various potential causes contributing to a problem. It acts as a visual tool that organizes potential causes of a problem into categories, facilitating a structured analysis process. These categories typically include "6Ms": Manpower, Machine, Method, Material, Measurement, and Environment. By brainstorming within each category, teams can identify various factors contributing to the problem and visualize their relationships.

The 6 M's represent different categories of potential causes when using the Fishbone Diagram method. While there isn't a strict order to follow, arranging them in a specific sequence catered to the situation can help ensure a comprehensive analysis and facilitate the identification of root causes. The main goal is to take each category and dissect each "M" by pinpointing all factors within each category that may be the potential culprit of the issue at hand.

Here's a suggested order:

1. **Manpower** (*People*): Start with understanding the people involved. This includes their skills, training, and how the organization works together. Look into things like whether they have the right training, if there are enough staff, or if there are any issues with communication.

2. **Machine** (*Equipment*): Next, check out the equipment and tools being used. This covers everything from machines to technology. See if there are any problems with equipment breaking down, not working properly, or if it's outdated.

3. **Method** (*Process*): Now, look at how things are done - the process. This includes the steps taken and how things are organized. Check if the process is efficient, if it needs updating, or if there are any inconsistencies.

4. **Material:** After that, focus on the materials being used. This involves looking at the quality of materials, whether they're available when needed, and if there are any problems with the supply chain.

5. **Measurement** (*Management*): Then, consider how things are measured and managed. This involves looking at metrics, data collection methods, and how performance is tracked. Check if there are any issues with measuring performance accurately, outdated ways of measuring, or if there's a lack of communication between managers, teams, and individuals.

6. **Environment:** Finally, think about the broader environment. This includes physical, social, and cultural factors outside the organization's control. Look at things like regulations, market conditions, workplace culture, and any external influences that could be impacting the problem.

By following these steps, you'll look at everything that could be causing the problem, both inside and outside the company. But remember, you can change the order or the specific M's used depending on the situation. Also, working together with different teams can help find causes more easily.

Even if you're not a company or business, you can still use the Fishbone Diagram to analyze problems professionally or individually. For example, if you're a freelancer experiencing a decline in clients, you can use the diagram to explore various factors contributing to this issue. Categories like "Skills," "Marketing," "Communication," "Networking," and "Time Management" can help you identify potential root causes. This visual tool can guide your thinking and help you develop targeted strategies to address the underlying issues.

Or let's say you're a student having trouble with time management and consistently missing deadlines. You can use the Fishbone Diagram to investigate the root causes of this problem. Using the Fishbone Diagram, you can explore the root causes of this issue. Start by identifying "Time Management" as the central cause, then delve into categories like "Study Environment" (noise distractions, lack of organization), "Study Habits" (procrastination, distractions), "External Commitments" (extracurricular activities, part-time jobs), "Technology Use" (social media distractions), and "Health and Well-being" (sleep, stress). This approach helps pinpoint the factors contributing to your challenges and guides you in developing targeted solutions to improve your time management skills.

In general, adapting the 6M's to the specific categories relevant to the problem at hand when utilizing the fishbone diagram unlocks its remarkable problem-solving potential. This tailored approach enables you to dissect complex issues effectively and identify actionable insights, facilitating the development of targeted solutions to address root causes and drive meaningful change.

FISHBONE DIAGRAM OUTLINE

Machine
- Equipment
- Machine

Method
- Process
- Efficiency

Measurement
- Management
- Metrics

Problem → Solution

Manpower
- People
- Schemes

Material
- Resources
- Supply

Environment
- External Factors
- Company Culture

The diagram's structure provides a visual analysis of the problem by prompting the team or individual to brainstorm and identify relevant factors within each category. By visualizing these potential causes and their relationships to the problem, one can better understand the underlying issues and develop targeted solutions to fix the problem quickly and effectively. Utilizing the Fishbone Diagram is a systematic approach that offers clarity and structure to problem-solving endeavors.

Here's a recap of the important steps to follow:

Step 1: Start by clearly defining the problem statement at the "tail" of the fishbone, providing a concise description of the issue at hand.

Step 2: Next, brainstorm and list potential causes under each category using the 6 M's (Manpower, Method, Machine, Material, Measurement, and Environment), adding more "bones" as needed to capture all possible factors.

Step 3: Analyze the relationships between the identified causes and the problem, delving into the root causes and contributing factors that could potentially resolve the issue.

Step 4: Prioritize the most critical causes for further investigation, planning, or immediate action, ensuring focused attention on key areas.

Step 5: Finally, develop and implement strategies to address the identified root causes, crafting solutions that mitigate the problem and lead to the desired outcome, symbolized by the "result" at the head of the fishbone.

FISHBONE DIAGRAM WITH EXAMPLE

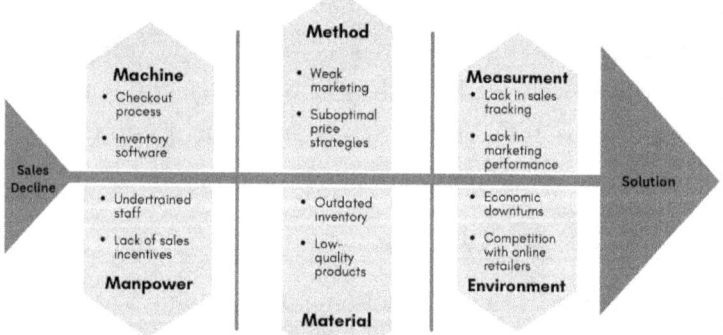

As you can see, using an example of a retail store with declining sales, the fishbone diagram serves as a valuable tool for problem-solving and root cause analysis. It facilitates a structured visual approach to identifying and addressing underlying issues within the organization or process that may be causing the decline in sales. This allows the retail store to properly follow the five steps and create a solution.

By following this systematic approach, teams and individuals can leverage the Fishbone Diagram to uncover root causes, devise targeted solutions, and foster continuous improvement in their operations. Through its visual clarity and structured methodology, the Fishbone Diagram empowers problem-solvers to navigate challenges effectively and drive positive change within their respective domains.

Selecting the Root Cause

After identifying potential root causes using tools such as the 5 Whys or Fishbone Diagram, the subsequent step of selecting the most probable root cause is pivotal. This decision forms the cornerstone of problem-solving efforts, as it directs the focus towards developing solutions that effectively target the underlying issues driving the problem.

By carefully choosing the most likely root cause, organizations and individuals can ensure that their resources and efforts are directed towards addressing the fundamental issues at hand, leading to more impactful and sustainable solutions.

The selection process involves evaluating each potential cause based on several criteria:

Relevance

Alignment with the Observed Problem - Each potential root cause must be assessed to determine its alignment with the observed problem. This involves evaluating the causal relationship between the identified cause and the observed symptoms or issues. A relevant root cause is one that directly contributes to the problem and can explain its cause.

Impact on Objectives - Furthermore, it's important to think about how each potential cause affects the goals you're aiming to achieve. For instance, if your goal is to improve a process, you'd want to focus on root causes that have the biggest impact on making that process better once solved. This ensures that your efforts are directed towards fixing the most important issues first, leading to better outcomes overall. Prioritizing causes that align directly with the problem's objectives ensures that resources are directed towards addressing issues with the most significant impact.

Feasibility

Practicality of Addressing the Root Cause - Assessing the feasibility of addressing each potential root cause involves considering practical factors such as resource availability, technical expertise, and time constraints. It's essential to evaluate whether a company or individual has the necessary resources, skills, and capabilities to effectively address the identified cause within a reasonable timeframe.

Resource Requirements - Additionally, consider the resource requirements associated with addressing each potential cause. This includes manpower, financial resources, technology, along with basic structures and facilities needed for operation. Prioritize causes that can be feasibly addressed given the constraints and resource limitations required to solve the issue at hand.

Potential Impact

Evaluation of Impact on Problem Resolution - Assessing the impact of addressing each root cause involves considering how much it will help solve the problem. Consider the potential effectiveness of addressing each cause in terms of reducing or eliminating the symptoms of the problem.

Desired Outcomes - Furthermore, consider the desired outcomes or objectives that your company or situation aims to achieve through problem resolution. Prioritize root causes that have the greatest potential to drive desired outcomes and contribute to achieving long-term goals once solved.

It's essential to select the root cause(s) that align most closely with the observed issue, are feasible to address, and have the potential to make a significant impact on problem resolution. It's always important to remember that improper root cause identification can lead to wasted time, resources, and confusion for everyone involved. Which is why utilizing the steps within the root cause identification process and its tools are crucial to all problem-solving situations. For instance, in the case of declining sales in a retail store, identifying the lack of budget allocation for market research as a root cause meets these criteria. This decision reflects its direct relevance to the problem, ability to evaluate feasibility within organizational constraints, and its potential impact on improving sales performance. By prioritizing such root causes, organizations can effectively direct their resources towards implementing solutions that lead to sustainable improvements.

Overall, systematically applying Root Cause Analysis techniques and evaluating potential root causes based on relevance, feasibility, and potential impact, organizations and individuals can gain valuable insights into the factors driving their problems. This structured approach enhances problem-solving capabilities, fosters a culture of continuous learning and improvement, and ultimately drives sustainable business success. It ensures that resources are directed towards addressing root causes effectively, leading to lasting solutions and improved organizational performance.

Part II: The Plan

Developing Countermeasures and Action Plans

If your only tool is a hammer then every problem looks like a nail.

- Abraham Maslow

The Plan

After identifying and understanding the root causes of a problem through techniques such as the 5 Whys or Fishbone Diagram, the next critical step in the problem-solving process is to develop countermeasures. Countermeasures are proactive strategies and actions aimed at addressing the root causes and mitigating the impact of the problem. In simpler terms, developing countermeasures and action plans means creating "actions" or "steps taken" to reduce a problem or prevent it from happening again.

This section will explore the process of developing countermeasures, including generating possible solutions, evaluating and prioritizing them, as well as creating actionable plans for taking action.

Generating Possible Solutions

Generating possible solutions involves brainstorming and exploring a range of strategies and interventions to address the identified root causes. This phase encourages creativity and different approaches, allowing you to consider various avenues and alternatives one can utilize to act on the problem. By fostering an environment where all ideas are welcomed and encouraged, teams and individuals can tap into diverse perspectives and experiences, potentially uncovering innovative solutions that might not have been considered otherwise. Generating a plethora of potential solutions allows you to explore a variety of options and consider unconventional or out-of-the-box approaches that can fix the problem at hand.

This Includes:

- Brainstorming sessions
- Benchmarking
- Pilot Programs
- Evaluating and prioritizing solutions

Let's evaluate these powerful and commonly used countermeasures. These will help form a concrete roadmap on how to approach a problem after the root cause has been determined and the potential solutions are ready to be implemented.

Brainstorming Sessions

Conducting brainstorming sessions is a dynamic and collaborative approach to generating a wide range of ideas and perspectives for problem solving. This can be done individually or within a team setting depending on the situation and its complexity.

Brainstorming helps create new ideas, polish old ones, and helps individuals work together effectively to find creative solutions to their problem-solving procedures. By harnessing the collective intelligence and creativity between individuals, brainstorming enables the exploration of innovative solutions to intricate problem-solving challenges.

Here's the brainstorming diagram (follow clockwise).

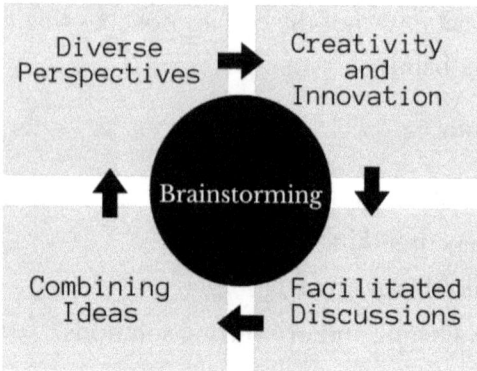

Let's dive deeper into brainstorming:

- **Diverse Perspectives:** By involving individuals from various departments or areas of expertise, brainstorming sessions harness the collective intelligence of everyone. Each participant brings a unique viewpoint and set of experiences to the table, expanding the pool of potential solutions.

- **Creativity and Innovation:** Brainstorming sessions provide a platform for creative thinking and innovation. Participants are encouraged to think outside the box, challenge assumptions, and explore unconventional approaches to problem-solving. This creative freedom often leads to breakthrough ideas and novel solutions that may not have been considered otherwise.

- **Facilitated Discussions:** Effective facilitation is essential for maximizing the impact of brainstorming sessions. A skilled facilitator creates a supportive environment where all voices are heard, ideas are valued, and participants feel empowered to contribute openly.

- **Combining Ideas:** Following the brainstorming session, it's essential to combine and organize the generated ideas for further evaluation. Group similar ideas together, prioritize those with the most potential impact or feasibility, and identify common themes or patterns that emerge. This process lays the groundwork for selecting and refining the most promising solutions.

As you can see, brainstorming, whether alone or in groups, is essential for unlocking creativity and generating innovative solutions. Even when brainstorming solo, individuals can draw upon their diverse experiences and perspectives to enrich their pool of potential solutions using the same exact guidelines and tailor them to their current situation.

By fostering a mindset of openness and challenging assumptions, individuals can stimulate creativity and explore unconventional approaches. While facilitated discussions may not be possible alone, self-reflection and critical evaluation can substitute, enabling individuals to objectively evaluate ideas and prioritize those with the most potential impact. Ultimately, whether alone or in a group, the goal of brainstorming remains consistent: to explore possibilities and generate innovative solutions to complex problems by opening the floodgates to creative thinking. That is the power brainstorming provides while using the A3 problem-solving model.

Benchmarking

Benchmarking involves researching and analyzing best practices, industry standards, and successful case studies from similar organizations or industries that can be used and implemented. Essentially, benchmarking is looking at what others are doing well and figuring out how to replicate it or do it better. It's about finding out what works for others and using those valuable insights to improve your own performance or practices.

Here's how you can leverage benchmarking effectively:

Learning from Others: Benchmarking allows you to learn from the successes and failures of others in similar contexts. By studying industry leaders and top performers, organizations can gain valuable insights into effective strategies, processes, and approaches to problem-solving.

For example, a small manufacturing company wants to improve its production efficiency. By benchmarking against industry leaders known for their efficient manufacturing processes, the company can study their production methods, equipment utilization rates, and workflow strategies. By learning from these successful companies, the manufacturing company can gain insights into how to optimize its own production processes and improve efficiency.

Identifying Best Practices: Through benchmarking, organizations can identify best practices that have proven effective in addressing similar problems or challenges. This may include innovative techniques, cutting-edge technologies, or novel approaches to business processes.

For instance, let's consider a fast-food chain like Chick-fil-A, renowned for its exceptional customer service. In striving to enhance its own customer experience, a competing fast-food chain might turn to Chick-fil-A as a benchmark. By studying Chick-fil-A's personalized interactions, efficient complaint handling, and smooth checkout processes, the competing chain can learn valuable insights to elevate its own customer service standards and stand out in the market.

Adapting: When looking to improve processes and systems, it's essential to adapt and tailor best practices to fit the organization's unique context, culture, and objectives.

However, what works for one organization may not necessarily work for another, so it's crucial to consider factors such as organizational size, industry dynamics, and resource constraints when adapting and searching for processes or systems that require improvement.

Let's use a healthcare clinic that wants to improve patient wait times. While benchmarking against other clinics can provide valuable insights on the matter, it's essential to consider the clinic's unique context, such as patient demographics, facility layout, and staff resources. The clinic adapts benchmarked best practices to fit its specific context, implementing strategies such as appointment scheduling optimization, workflow redesign, and staff training tailored to address its challenges and constraints.

Continuous Improvement: Benchmarking is not a one-time activity but rather an ongoing process of continuous improvement. Organizations and individuals should regularly review and update their benchmarking efforts to stay abreast of industry trends, emerging best practices, and evolving market conditions. Continuous improvement is the key to keeping an organization or business afloat and at the top of the competitive food chain.

Pilot Programs

A pilot program, also known as a pilot project or pilot initiative, is a small-scale, limited-duration experiment or "test run" to measure the feasibility, effectiveness, and potential impact of a proposed solution or intervention in a real-world setting. Pilot programs are typically implemented before launching a new initiative, product, or service across the entire organization or target audience.

Think of it as a test drive for a new vehicle purchase, you want to know if the vehicle will fulfill your needs before swiping your card and making a big commitment. Pilot programs act as a smaller-scale trial or test phase allowing organizations or individuals to assess how the solution performs in practice, gather feedback, and identify any necessary adjustments or refinements before rolling out the final procedure. This can include things such as a company implementing a new customer service initiative and observing its efficiency, testing a new product and its attractiveness to the target audience, or even sampling a new marketing method to measure its effectiveness before investing in a marketing campaign.

Here's why pilot programs are valuable:

Risk Mitigation: Pilot programs allow you to mitigate risks associated with implementing new solutions on a large scale. By testing solutions in a controlled environment, organizations and individuals can identify and address potential challenges, uncertainties, and unintended consequences before rolling them out more broadly.

Gathering Real-World Data: Pilot programs provide an opportunity to gather real-world data and feedback on the feasibility and effectiveness of different approaches. By collecting quantitative and qualitative data during the pilot phase, organizations can evaluate the impact of the solution, identify areas for improvement, and make informed decisions based on evidence.

Involving Key Participants: Involving key participants such as employees, customers, or stakeholders in pilot programs fosters engagement, ownership, and buy-in for the proposed solutions. Key participants have an opportunity to provide input, share insights, and contribute to the refinement of the solution based on their experiences and perspectives.

Iterative Learning: Pilot programs facilitate iterative learning and continuous improvement. Organizations can use the insights gained from the pilot phase to refine and optimize the solution iteratively, increasing its effectiveness and maximizing its impact over time.

Let's delve into an example where an organization initiates a pilot program to assess the effectiveness of a new customer service initiative geared towards enhancing response times to customer inquiries. This hypothetical scenario offers insight into the practical application of forming a pilot program within an organizational context.

Keep in mind that you have the flexibility to tailor and refine this sample outline to align with the specific requirements and objectives of your unique problem-solving endeavor. The main goal is to form a plan, test its effectiveness, and evaluate any necessary adjustments after.

1. **Introduction and Problem Statement**

    - Definition: Begin by introducing the purpose of the pilot program and the specific problem or challenge it aims to address.

    - Example: In a customer service initiative, introduce the problem of long wait times for customer inquiries and the negative impact it has on customer satisfaction and retention.

2. Objectives and Goals

- Definition: Clearly outline the objectives and goals of the pilot program, highlighting what success looks like after a solution has been implemented.

- Example: Set the objective to reduce customer inquiry response times by 50% within three months, aiming to enhance customer satisfaction scores by 20%.

3. Scope and Timeline

- Definition: Define the scope of the pilot program, including the any specific areas or processes it will cover, along with a realistic timeline for the implementation of potential solutions.

- Example: Scope the pilot program to focus on improving response times for email inquiries initially, with a timeline of three months for implementation and evaluation.

4. Key Performance Indicators (KPIs)

- Definition: Establish measurable KPIs to track the effectiveness and impact of the pilot program.

- Example: KPIs may include average response time to customer inquiries, customer satisfaction scores, and retention rates before and after implementation.

5. Implementation Plan

- Definition: Develop a detailed plan outlining the steps and actions required to implement the pilot program successfully. This also includes any new training, technology, or processes required to implement the pilot program.

- Example: Implement a new email management system with automated routing and prioritization features, provide training to customer service representatives on effective communication and problem-solving techniques, and establish regular monitoring and feedback mechanisms.

6. Resource Allocation

- Definition: Allocate the necessary resources, including budget, personnel, and technology, to support the implementation of the pilot program.

- Example: Allocate funds for acquiring and implementing the new email management system, designate staff members to undergo training and lead the initiative and ensure access to necessary technology and tools.

7. Risk Management

- Definition: Identify potential risks and challenges that may arise during the pilot program and develop strategies to mitigate them.

- Example: Anticipate the risk of technical glitches or resistance to change from staff members and develop contingency plans, such as providing additional technical support or offering incentives for participation.

8. **Evaluation and Feedback Mechanisms**

    - Definition: Establish processes for ongoing evaluation and feedback to monitor the progress of the pilot program and make necessary adjustments.

    - Example: Implement regular surveys or feedback forms for customers to provide input on their experience, conduct weekly check-ins with staff members to address any issues or concerns, and analyze KPIs to track progress towards objectives.

9. **Documentation and Reporting**

    - Definition: Document all aspects of the pilot program, including implementation activities, outcomes, and lessons learned, and prepare reports to communicate findings to key participants.

    - Example: Maintain detailed records of email response times, customer feedback, and any changes made during the pilot program, and prepare a comprehensive report summarizing the results and recommendations for future actions. Utilizing this data ensures the program works or needs further adjustments.

10. Scale-up

- Definition: Develop a plan for scaling up successful elements of the pilot program to the broader organization or applying lessons learned to similar initiatives in the future.

- Example: If the pilot program successfully reduces email response times and improves customer satisfaction, develop a plan to implement similar strategies across all customer service channels and explore opportunities to apply the same approach to other areas of the organization, such as technical support or sales. This allows the company to scale their tested solutions within the entire organization, providing valuable change.

By following these steps, the company can efficiently establish and execute pilot programs, enabling them to test new strategies, acquire data-driven insights, and foster ongoing enhancements in customer service and various operational aspects. Depending on the situation and the nature of the problem being addressed, you can choose all approaches or choose the approach that best suits your needs and resources.

Whether you're an entrepreneur launching a new product, a company leader seeking to optimize internal systems, or a professional aiming to refine personal workflows, implementing pilot programs can be a valuable approach to innovation and improvement. It allows you to test, refine, and confidently choose any aspects of the plan that will successfully implement and scale the solution.

Evaluating and Prioritizing Solutions

Once a healthy range of potential solutions has been brainstormed, benchmarked, and piloted, the next crucial step is to evaluate and prioritize them. This ensures that resources are directed effectively towards the most promising solutions first. This requires measuring the feasibility, potential impact, and alignment with objectives.

Here's a simplified guide on how to carry out this process followed by an example of our customer service initiative scenario:

Feasibility

Assess and prioritize the feasibility of each potential solution(s) and the resources required for implementation, considering factors such as time, cost, technical expertise, and organizational capabilities. This step ensures that the chosen solution is realistic and achievable within your current capabilities at that moment in time. Which allows you to start making positive changes immediately and prepare for further action later.

For instance, improving internal communication processes for the company first is a more feasible initial step because it requires less investment of resources like time and money. This approach allows an organization to make immediate improvements within their customer initiative while preparing for more extensive improvements in the future that cost more money or require in-depth technical expertise.

Potential Impact

Evaluate the potential impact of each solution on addressing the root causes of the problem and achieving desired outcomes. Prioritize solutions that have the greatest potential to bring about positive change and address the core issues.

For example, implementing streamlined communication channels to start directly targets the identified root cause of customer service inefficiency. This solution is likely to have a significant impact on improving response times and overall customer satisfaction immediately while preparing for further action later on that requires more resources.

Alignment with Objectives

Consider how well each solution aligns with the strategic goals, values, and priorities of the organization. Prioritize solutions that support long-term objectives and contribute to the overall success of the company and anyone who may be involved.

Solutions that enhance customer satisfaction and strengthen customer relationships are aligned with the objective of providing exceptional customer service and driving customer loyalty. Therefore, they should be given high priority in the decision-making process. Once its implementation is successful, further implementation can be incorporated.

In summary, evaluating and prioritizing solutions involves assessing their feasibility, potential impact, and alignment with objectives. By strategically focusing on solutions that are practical, impactful, and aligned with long-term goals, organizations can effectively address problems and drive positive change even if further action is required later.

Creating Your Action Plans

Once potential solutions have been evaluated, prioritized, and tested, it's time to create concrete action plans for their implementation. They serve as roadmaps for executing solutions, allocating resources, setting timelines, and monitoring progress towards achieving desired outcomes once you're ready to fully act on the problem.

Creating action plans is like plotting a course on a map before a journey, outlining clear objectives and strategies to navigate challenges and reach the desired destination effectively. In the upcoming Part III of this book, we'll delve into this section with a more detailed and structured approach, enabling you to articulate your action plans effectively in one place. For now, we will go over the necessary guidelines for creating action plans, accompanied by an example from our customer service initiative scenario to further elaborate.

Here are the four steps to creating action plans:

1. **Specific Goals and Objectives**
   - Definition: Clearly define the goals and objectives of each solution, including desired outcomes and success criteria.
   - Example: For instance, the goal of the company implementing streamlined communication channels is to reduce response times by 20% within three months and to improve customer satisfaction ratings by 15% within six months.

2. **Implementation Steps**
   - Definition: Outline all the specific steps and tasks needed to implement each solution, along with responsibilities and deadlines required for implementation.
   - Example: To implement the plan, the company may need to create new training materials and designate duties to organizational leaders responsible for conducting the training along with feasible deadlines to have employees trained by.

3. **Resource Allocation**
   - Definition: Identify the resources, budget, and support required for successful implementation. Allocate resources effectively to support implementation efforts.

- Example: This may involve allocating funds for training programs and ongoing support for the company.

4. Monitoring and Evaluation

- Definition: Set up ways to measure and track how well each solution is working. Keep an eye on progress and see if it's making a difference. This includes establishing metrics and key performance indicators (KPIs) to measure the effectiveness and impact of each solution.

- Example: Metrics may include evaluating the result of response times, customer satisfaction scores, and resolution rates based on the specific goals and objectives set for the company.

Although creating action plans may seem very similar to formulating pilot programs, they each have their own purpose and should be followed respectfully due to their individual functionality. Creating an action plan involves detailing the steps, responsibilities, timelines, and resources needed to implement chosen countermeasures or solutions. Implementing a pilot program, on the other hand, entails testing potential solutions on a small scale before broader implementation to evaluate effectiveness and gather feedback.

To conclude Part II, by systematically constructing countermeasures, evaluating, prioritizing, and creating detailed actionable plans for implementation, organizations and individuals can translate insights from root cause analysis into effective strategies for improvement in which they can successfully take action on. This structured approach enhances problem-solving capabilities, fosters innovation and collaboration, and ultimately drives sustainable business success. Now, it's time to consolidate all the information gathered during the A3 process along with our planned solutions and put them into action.

Part III: Mastering A3 Methodology

Structuring an A3 report, Implementing, and Follow-up

Action is the foundational key to all success.

- Pablo Picasso

Mastering A3 Methodology

Now that we have fully explored the process of understanding the problem, identifying root causes, and developing countermeasures with action plans, it is imperative to put it all together by creating and executing the *A3 report*.

This section will provide you with the essential framework for encapsulating the entirety of the problem's situation and proficiently implementing countermeasures. Furthermore, we will discuss the significance of diligent follow-up procedures, ensuring the efficiency of the implemented solutions, and facilitating necessary adjustments to address any lingering issues.

The A3 Report

The A3 report is a powerful tool utilized by organizations to streamline problem-solving processes and facilitate effective communication of solutions. Its name stems from the standard paper size used for its layout, emphasizing the need for concise and comprehensive documentation.

Whether created on a physical sheet of paper or through digital platforms like Microsoft Word or PowerPoint, the A3 report serves as a visual representation of the problem, analysis, and proposed solutions. The A3 report facilitates a linear approach to problem-solving, guiding everyone through the process from problem identification to solution implementation. Its versatility allows for easy sharing of information across teams and individuals promoting healthy collaboration and alignment in problem-solving efforts.

To ensure the effectiveness of the A3 report, it is essential to focus on clarity and brevity, condensing any complex information into a format that is easily understandable and actionable for all key participants involved. This promotes consistency and efficiency in problem-solving efforts, ultimately leading to more effective outcomes.

A3 Report Outline

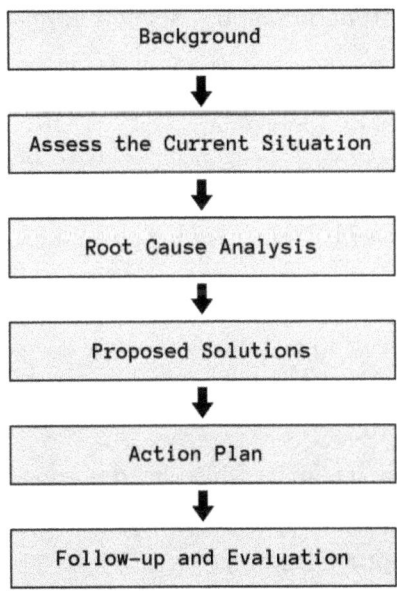

Following the provided outline above, the A3 Report consists of six key sections (or steps) that are essential in bringing everything together. By following these steps, organizations and individuals can articulate the entirety of the problem and its solution(s) with ease.

Background – Section One

- Clearly articulate the problem or challenge you're addressing.

- Explain its significance and impact on your organization, team, or personal goals.

- Provide any necessary context or background information to set the stage.

Asses the Current Situation – Section Two

- Gather and analyze relevant data and observations related to the problem.

- Use quantitative metrics, qualitative feedback, and process observations to capture the current state.

- Highlight key pain points, inefficiencies, or issues that need to be addressed.

Root Cause Analysis – Section Three

- Describe and/or illustrate the root causes of the problem created by tools such as the 5 Whys or Fishbone Diagram.

- This section helps articulate the underlying factors driving the problem.

Proposed Solutions - Section Four

- State the potential countermeasures or solutions to address the identified root causes.

- Disclose the best benchmarking practices and potential pilot programs.

- Share research that proposes innovative approaches in relation to your planned solution

- For each proposed solution, clearly define the rationale, expected outcomes, and any potential risks or challenges.

Action Plan - Section Five

- Outline the specific implementation steps for each proposed solution.

- Assign responsibilities, deadlines, and resource requirements for each step.

- Define key performance indicators (KPIs) or metrics to measure the success of each solution.

- Establish a feasible timeline for the entire plan to be carried out by.

- Establish a monitoring plan for tracking progress and adjusting as needed.

Follow-up and Evaluation – Section Six

- Outline how progress will be monitored, evaluated, and communicated following the implementation of the solutions.

- This ensures accountability and continuous improvement on any necessary adjustments.

- Rinse and repeat until the problem is successfully mitigated or fully resolved.

Elements of a Good A3 Report

Crafting an A3 report can indeed feel daunting due to the intricate nature of problem-solving and solution implementation depending on its complexity. However, by incorporating these essential elements, one can streamline the process and ensure clarity, brevity, and effectiveness in communication. Here's some guidance on vital components that can be implemented into your A3 report, enhancing its overall quality and impact.

A well-crafted A3 report should possess these five elements:

1. **Clarity:** Ensure that the report is clear, concise, and easy to understand. Use plain language and avoid jargon to communicate effectively with all key participants.

2. **Visuals:** Incorporate visuals when needed such as charts, graphs, and diagrams to enhance understanding and illustrate key points. Visuals help to convey complex information in a more digestible format.

3. **Logical Flow**: Organize the report in a logical sequence, with each section building upon the previous one. This facilitates comprehension and guides the reader through the problem-solving process.

4. **Data-driven**: Base your analysis and recommendations on data and facts rather than assumptions or opinions. This adds credibility to the report and helps justify proposed solutions.

5. **Engagement**: Seek input and feedback throughout the problem-solving process from others that can provide valuable insight on the problem and its potential solutions. This fosters useful advice, collaboration, and ownership of the solutions.

Tips for Effective Communication

When implementing the A3 problem-solving method with a team, effective communication is essential for ensuring the A3 report's success. Similar to the five elements, these tips will help tremendously while working with others.

Here are some tips to enhance communication:

1. **Know Your Audience**: Tailor the A3 report to the needs and preferences of your audience. Consider their level of expertise, interests, and concerns when crafting the report. It's important to make sure that everyone involved can understand the problem and its solution.

2. **Use Plain Language**: Avoid technical jargon and acronyms that may be unfamiliar to the reader. Use simple, straightforward language to properly convey your message clearly.

3. **Tell a Story**: Frame the problem-solving process as a narrative, highlighting the journey from identifying the problem to implementing solutions. Engage the reader by weaving a compelling story that resonates with them.

4. **Seek Feedback**: Encourage feedback from key participants throughout the problem-solving process. This can include team members, stakeholders, or anyone who can provide valuable insights and feedback. Actively listen to their input and perspectives.

5. **Follow Up**: After presenting the A3 report, follow up with key participants to ensure understanding and address any questions or concerns. After the report has been implemented, keep them informed of progress and incorporate any adjustments.

6. **Troubleshooting**: Addressing issues such as resistance to change or overcoming communication barriers requires empathy, active listening, and clear articulation of benefits. Understand concerns, provide support, and involve individuals in decision-making to foster ownership and commitment. Being patient, persistent, and relatable in efforts to facilitate a smooth transition is key.

By adhering to these principles and guidelines, you can create an A3 report that effectively communicates the problem-solving process and proposed solutions. This structured approach enhances collaboration, fosters alignment, and drives continuous improvement. Now that we've covered how to create an A3 report, let's dive into how to implement and follow-up in more detail.

Implementation and Follow-up

Once the A3 report has been created and solutions have been identified, the next critical step is to implement these countermeasures effectively. A3 report implementation involves putting the proposed solutions into action, monitoring progress, and adjusting as needed. This will be done in a team setting, or, if you are individually executing, you will be implementing the report yourself. Let's explore how to carry out this process.

Here's how to approach implementation:

Action Plan Execution: Follow the action plan outlined in the A3 report to carry out the proposed solutions. Assign responsibilities, set deadlines, and allocate resources as needed to ensure smooth execution. If new issues arise during the process, address any roadblocks promptly by identifying root causes and conducting brainstorming solutions on the matter.

Clear Communication: Communicate the implementation plan to all relevant key participants, ensuring everyone understands their roles and responsibilities, and always seek consistent feedback from them during the process. Clear communication fosters accountability and ensures alignment towards achieving the desired outcomes.

If communication is solo based, this can be done internally via documented notes or within the A3 report. Either way will provide clear instructions for the plan's execution in a successful manner.

Training and Support: Provide training and support to individuals involved in implementing countermeasures, especially if new processes or technologies are being introduced. This ensures that everyone has the necessary skills and knowledge to execute their tasks effectively.

If the training and support is solo based, prepare and implement any necessary training needed for countermeasure implementation and have anyone who can provide support on standby such as a mentor or trusted colleague who can provide valuable input.

Overall, implementing countermeasures entails executing the action plan with clear responsibilities, deadlines, and resource allocation. For team implementation, clear communication among all key participants ensures alignment and accountability for everyone. For solo implementation, clear communication within the A3 report to oneself or with external support is just as important. Additionally, providing adequate training and support to anyone involved in the implementation will ensure successful execution.

Monitoring Progress

Monitoring progress, also known as following up, is essential to track the effectiveness of the implemented countermeasures and identify any areas that require attention. The importance of monitoring progress cannot be overstated, as it serves as a feedback loop that informs decision-making and adjustment of strategies. Without ongoing monitoring, there is a risk of overlooking emerging issues or failing to capitalize on opportunities for improvement. Additionally, monitoring progress while the plan is in motion helps maintain accountability and transparency within organizations or individuals. It allows all participants to see the tangible impact over time.

Here's how to monitor progress effectively:

Establish Metrics: Define all key performance indicators (KPIs) and metrics to measure the impact of the implemented solutions. These may include metrics such as response times, increase in sales numbers, customer satisfaction scores, defect rates, or even website traffic depending on the nature of the business and the problem being addressed.

Whether you're tracking metrics by quantitative or qualitative value, the main goal is to ensure there are improvements happening and that the metrics align directly with your overall objective.

Regular Data Collection: Collect data regularly to track progress against the established metrics. Use data collection methods such as factual observations, reports, surveys, interviews, or automated systems used that can gather relevant information.

Data Analysis: Analyze the collected data to identify trends, patterns, and areas for improvement. Overall, data analysis is a critical component of monitoring progress and driving continuous improvement. Keep an eye out for things not going as planned and figure out why they're happening to fix any other unexpected problems along the way.

Adjusting Strategies as Needed

Continuous improvement is at the core of A3 problem-solving methodology. Adjusting strategies based on monitoring results ensures agility and responsiveness to changing conditions. The solutions implemented may not yield the results you want at first. Just as a skilled sailor adjusts their course based on changing currents and obstacles, so too must problem solvers adapt their strategies to overcome challenges and steer towards their desired outcomes.

Here's three ways on how to adjust strategies effectively:

1. **Review and Reflect:** Regularly review all and any progress against the established metrics and reflect on the effectiveness of the implemented countermeasures. Consider whether the desired outcomes are being achieved and whether adjustments are needed.

2. **Root Cause Analysis:** If progress is not meeting expectations, conduct additional root cause analysis to under-

stand the underlying reasons for performance gaps. This may involve revisiting the problem-solving process and identifying new solutions or refining existing ones.

3. **Iterative Approach:** Take an iterative approach to problem-solving, making incremental adjustments based on feedback and learning from past experiences. Always take small steps, embrace gradual improvements, and be willing to adapt if needed.

In summary, Part III emphasizes the importance of implementing countermeasures effectively, monitoring progress, and adapting as needed. By following this calculated implementation approach to problem-solving, both organizations and individuals can foster continuous improvement and attain sustainable results.

This approach enables flexibility in responding to changing circumstances and ensures a loyal commitment to delivering value. If you encounter challenges during the adjustment process, don't hesitate to seek guidance from key participants or trusted mentors who can offer valuable insights and advice tailored to your specific situation.

Remember, embracing a mindset of continuous learning and adaptation is key to overcoming obstacles and achieving long-term success. Without it, organizations and individuals will find themselves in a constant circle of confusion and frustration with every problem or obstacle along the way. Because of that, it's imperative to always maintain an adaptive mindset and find motivation to continue learning and improving. As time passes and new problems arise, you will be prepared and ready to take on any hurdle that comes your way as a result. Embracing a mindset of continuous learning and adaptation empowers you to stay ahead of the curve, drive continuous improvement, and achieve long-term success in the ever-changing world we live in today.

Part IV: Extras

Case Studies,

Continuous Improvement,

and Beyond

Without continual growth and progress, such words as improvement, achievement, and success have no meaning.

- Benjamin Franklin

Extras

In this section of the book, we delve into the practical application of A3 problem-solving methodologies through real-world examples, showcasing successful implementations and extracting valuable insights from each case study. By examining these examples, readers can gain a deeper understanding of how A3 methodology is effectively utilized in various contexts, from manufacturing to healthcare to project management.

Moreover, we explore the crucial aspect of fostering a culture of continuous improvement within organizations and among individuals. Through integrating A3 problem-solving into daily operations, organizations can nurture a mindset of innovation, collaboration, and adaptability, driving sustainable growth and success.

Finally, we'll discuss recommendations for advanced techniques and books that complement the A3 methodology, offering readers additional tools and strategies to further enhance their problem-solving abilities. By equipping you with comprehensive learning resources, you can empower yourself to continue the journey of improvement and mastery in problem-solving. Now, let's turn the page and dive in!

CASE STUDIES

Toyota's Production Process Improvement

In Toyota's pursuit of manufacturing excellence, they encountered significant quality issues and inefficiencies within their vehicle production process, leading to defects and escalated costs. To address these challenges, Toyota embarked on a systematic problem-solving journey, beginning with a meticulous identification of specific areas where defects occurred, and processes were inefficient. This initial phase laid the groundwork for a comprehensive root cause analysis, where Toyota employed tools like the 5 Whys and Fishbone Diagrams to delve deep into the underlying reasons behind the identified issues. Through this analysis, they uncovered a range of factors contributing to the problems, including machine breakdowns, operator errors, and disruptions within the supply chain.

With a crystal-clear understanding of the root causes, Toyota set out to devise innovative solutions that would not only address the immediate issues but also foster long-term improvements in efficiency and quality. Embracing the principles of kaizen, or continuous improvement, Toyota empowered frontline workers to propose and implement solutions consistently. This collaborative approach led to the introduction of initiatives such as just-in-time (JIT) inventory systems, total quality management (TQM) practices, and jidoka (automation with human intelligence), all aimed at streamlining operations and enhancing overall quality.

Implementation of the proposed solutions was a pivotal phase in Toyota's problem-solving journey. Emphasizing the importance of hands-on observation and direct engagement with the processes, Toyota fostered a culture of genchi genbutsu, where decisions were grounded in actual observations rather than assumptions. This approach ensured that improvements were not only theoretically sound but also practical and effective in real-world scenarios. Through meticulous planning and execution, Toyota successfully integrated the proposed solutions into their production processes, leading to tangible improvements in various aspects of production.

The results of Toyota's A3 problem-solving initiatives were nothing short of remarkable. With a relentless dedication to continuous improvement and active involvement of employees at all levels, Toyota witnessed a significant reduction in defects and a remarkable increase in overall efficiency. Defects were slashed by 90%, and assembly time was halved, highlighting the transformative impact of their structured problem-solving approach.

Through this case study, Toyota exemplifies the power of embracing a culture of continuous improvement, empowering employees, and basing decisions on empirical evidence to achieve operational excellence in manufacturing.

Key Takeaways from Toyota

Thorough Problem Identification: Toyota's situation underscores the importance of identifying problems comprehensively and laying a strong foundation for effective problem-solving.

Root Cause Analysis: Toyota's use of tools like the 5 Whys and Fishbone Diagrams highlights the significance of delving deep into underlying factors to address fundamental issues.

Innovative Countermeasures: Toyota's approach emphasizes the importance of crafting innovative solutions and fostering a culture of continuous improvement.

Hands-On Implementation: Toyota's emphasis on practical execution with hands-on observation highlights the need for solutions to be not only theoretically sound but also practical and effective in real-world scenarios.

Source - Toyota's Production Process Improvement: Toyota Production System: Beyond Large-Scale Production by Taiichi Ohno.

Denver Health's Patient Flow Improvement

In addressing the challenges of patient flow, Denver Health, a significant healthcare system, confronted inefficiencies resulting in extended wait times and overcrowding within its emergency department, ultimately impacting patient satisfaction and overall operational effectiveness.

Employing the A3 problem-solving methodology, Denver Health embarked on a comprehensive root cause analysis. Their investigation revealed several critical contributors to the problem, including inefficiencies in the admission process such as delays in registration and triage, a lack of coordination and communication among departments, and inefficient bed management leading to delays in patient transfers.

To combat these issues, Denver Health developed a series of countermeasures through the A3 process. These included streamlining admission protocols and implementing electronic tracking systems to reduce bottlenecks, improving communication and handoffs between departments through standardized protocols and regular interdepartmental meetings, and implementing a real-time bed tracking system to enhance bed management and patient flow.

Implementation of these solutions was facilitated by the formation of cross-functional teams comprising representatives from various departments, including the emergency department, inpatient units, nursing staff, and hospital leadership. The precise implementation process encompassed training staff on new admission protocols and electronic tracking systems, establishing regular interdepartmental meetings and communication channels, and deploying the real-time bed tracking system while ensuring staff were adequately trained in its use.

Through the diligent execution of these countermeasures developed via the A3 problem-solving process, Denver Health achieved significant results. They saw a reduction in patient wait times in the emergency department by over 50%, along with improved patient satisfaction scores related to wait times and overall experience. Furthermore, there was enhanced operational efficiency and coordination among departments, leading to optimized bed management and patient flow throughout the healthcare system.

Key Takeaways from Denver Health

Comprehensive Problem Analysis: Denver Health's case underscores the importance of conducting a thorough root cause analysis to identify key contributors to the problem, highlighting the significance of understanding the problem's scope and underlying factors.

Strategic Countermeasure Development: Denver Health's use of the A3 process emphasizes the importance of developing targeted countermeasures tailored to address specific issues identified during the root cause analysis phase.

Cross-Functional Collaboration: Denver Health's approach highlights the value of cross-functional collaboration in implementing solutions, showcasing the importance of involving representatives from various departments to ensure comprehensive problem-solving efforts.

Measurable Results: Denver Health's success in achieving tangible results, such as reduced patient wait times and improved satisfaction scores, demonstrates the effectiveness of structured problem-solving methodologies like A3 in driving positive outcomes in complex healthcare settings.

Source: Denver Health Case Study, Institute for Healthcare Improvement

Accenture's Project Management Optimization

In Accenture's pursuit of operational excellence, they encountered challenges within their project management processes that hindered efficient project delivery and client satisfaction. Through the application of the A3 problem-solving methodology, Accenture embarked on a structured journey to address these issues and drive meaningful improvements.

Accenture's initial assessment revealed several key issues plaguing their project management practices. These included unclear communication of project scope, inefficient resource allocation, and a lack of standardized project management practices across different teams and projects. These issues not only impacted project timelines but also jeopardized client satisfaction and overall operational efficiency.

Utilizing the A3 problem-solving process, Accenture conducted a thorough root cause analysis to delve deeper into the underlying factors contributing to the identified problems. They examined various aspects of their project management processes, from initial client engagement to project execution, to identify critical pain points and inefficiencies. Through this analysis, they uncovered the root causes of issues such as miscommunication, resource mismanagement, and inconsistent project management methodologies.

Armed with insights from their root cause analysis, Accenture developed targeted countermeasures to address the identified issues. These included implementing a standardized project management framework that clearly defined project scopes, objectives, and deliverables. Additionally, they enhanced communication protocols to ensure transparency and alignment among project key participants. Accenture also deployed resource management tools to optimize resource allocation and utilization across projects, ensuring that teams had the necessary support to deliver projects efficiently and effectively.

Accenture executed their proposed solutions with precision and dedication, leveraging the A3 process to guide the implementation process. They rolled out the standardized project management framework across their project teams, providing training and support to ensure adoption and adherence to new practices. Communication protocols were reinforced through regular meetings, updates, and feedback sessions, fostering a culture of collaboration and accountability. Resource management tools were integrated into existing project management systems, enabling teams to allocate resources effectively and track utilization in real-time.

The implementation of powerful A3-driven solutions yielded significant improvements for Accenture's project management processes. Project delivery times were streamlined, with projects consistently meeting or exceeding client expectations. Client satisfaction rates saw a notable uptick as communication improved, and project outcomes became more aligned with client objectives. Additionally, operational efficiency across project teams improved, with standardized practices leading to better resource utilization and project outcomes. Through their commitment to continuous improvement and structured problem-solving, Accenture achieved tangible results that propelled their project management capabilities to new heights.

Key Takeaways from Accenture

Systematic Problem Identification: Accenture's case emphasizes the importance of systematically identifying key issues within project management processes, highlighting the need for a structured approach to problem identification to address challenges effectively.

Root Cause Analysis: Accenture's use of the A3 methodology underscores the significance of conducting thorough root cause analysis to uncover underlying factors contributing to operational inefficiencies, showcasing the value of delving deep into the root causes of problems to drive meaningful improvements.

Tailored Countermeasure Development: Accenture's approach highlights the importance of developing targeted countermeasures tailored to address specific issues identified during the root cause analysis phase, demonstrating the effectiveness of implementing solutions aligned with identified root causes.

Precise Implementation: Accenture's achievement in implementing A3-driven solutions underscores the criticality of precise and dedicated execution. This success emphasizes the necessity for meticulous planning and implementation to guarantee the successful adoption and integration of proposed solutions. Through careful execution, Accenture was able to ensure that the solutions were effectively implemented, contributing to the overall success of their problem-solving initiatives. This highlights the importance of attention to detail and commitment to execution in achieving desired outcomes.

Source: Accenture Case Study, Project Management Institute

Lessons Learned from Case Studies

Through successful A3 implementations, valuable lessons have emerged, offering insights that resonate with individuals at all levels. Let's delve into these lessons, crafted not just for the boardroom elite but for everyone striving to navigate the complexities of problem-solving in their journey.

From leadership commitment to employee empowerment and the power of data-driven decision-making, these lessons offer a roadmap for anyone looking to tackle obstacles head-on and drive meaningful change.

Leadership Commitment

Whether you're the CEO of a multinational corporation, a startup entrepreneur, or a professional individual, committing to A3 problem-solving is key. It's about championing the adoption of A3 methodologies and providing the necessary resources, training, and guidance to ensure success. Your dedication sets the tone for the entire situation and paves the way for effective problem-solving.

Empowerment

In any organization, empowering employees at all levels is vital for A3 initiatives to thrive. As a leader, it's about fostering an environment where everyone feels empowered to participate in problem-solving processes.

Empowerment is not limited to employees alone; it extends to individuals at every level, including solo entrepreneurs or professionals tackling challenges on their own.

It's about fostering an environment where everyone feels empowered to participate in problem-solving processes. Whether you're leading a team or working solo, tapping into your own expertise and creativity, or that of your team, is essential for driving impactful solutions.

Data-Driven Decision Making

Whether you're analyzing data in a corporate setting, poring over metrics as an individual entrepreneur, or analyzing sales data as a store manager, data is your guiding light in A3 problem-solving. Prioritizing data collection, analysis, and interpretation helps uncover root causes and informs targeted interventions. From corporate boardrooms to home offices, leveraging data ensures that decisions are grounded in evidence and lead to meaningful outcomes.

Cultivating a Culture of Continuous Improvement

Cultivating a Culture of Continuous Improvement is not just about implementing changes but fostering an environment where improvement becomes a natural part of the organizational DNA. It starts with leaders championing the importance of continuous improvement, consistently reinforcing its value, and leading by example. When leaders actively support and participate in improvement initiatives, it sends a powerful message throughout the organization, encouraging others to do the same.

When working within a company, empowering employees to contribute ideas is another essential aspect of building this culture. By creating channels for feedback and idea-sharing, organizations tap into the collective intelligence of their workforce. This not only generates innovative solutions but also fosters a sense of ownership and commitment among employees. The same principles apply for solo individuals, confiding in credible peers or mentors to share feedback with continually provides the same positive benefits.

Moreover, fostering a learning mindset is crucial. One should encourage curiosity, experimentation, and a willingness to challenge the status quo. When employees feel encouraged to try new approaches and learn from both successes and failures, it fuels a culture of continuous improvement. Embracing failure as a learning opportunity is perhaps one of the most critical factors. Instead of viewing failure as a setback, you should see it as a steppingstone to improvement. By reframing failures as valuable lessons, organizations and individuals can encourage risk-taking and innovation without the fear of repercussions.

Overall, building a culture of continuous improvement requires a multifaceted approach that involves leadership commitment, employee empowerment, a learning mindset, and a willingness to embrace failure. When you prioritize these elements alongside the A3 process, they create an environment where improvement becomes not just a goal but a way of life. From there, any problem that arises becomes manageable and solutions become easier to find no matter the situation and its complexities.

Integrating A3 into Daily Operations

To realize the benefits of A3 problem-solving, organizations and individuals must integrate it into their daily operations and instill habit-forming capabilities until the process has become second nature for all participants.

This involves:

- **Standardizing Processes:** Establishing standardized processes for problem identification, analysis, solution development, and implementation ensures consistency and repeatability. By formulating clear, crisp guidelines and templates for A3 reports and problem-solving methodologies, you can streamline the problem-solving process and drive efficiency.

- **Training and Development:** Providing training and development opportunities for employees and key participants on A3 problem-solving techniques and methodologies is essential. Organizations should invest in training programs, workshops, and coaching sessions to equip employees with the skills and knowledge needed to effectively apply A3 problem-solving principles in their daily work.

Solo individuals, including entrepreneurs and professionals, can implement continuous improvement principles by self-educating through resources like books and online courses. They should experiment with new approaches, seek feedback, and reflect on outcomes to refine their methods.

- **Continuous Monitoring and Review:** By regularly monitoring and reviewing A3 problem-solving initiatives, it allows you to track progress, identify areas for improvement, and make course corrections as needed. By establishing feedback loops and performance metrics, organizations and individuals can ensure that A3 problem-solving remains an integral part of their ongoing improvement efforts.

In the case of unexpected roadblocks or issues along the way, here are some troubleshooting tips to follow:

Ensure Alignment - Regularly assess whether the standardized processes align with organizational or individual goals and objectives. Adjust as necessary to maintain relevance and effectiveness.

Enhance Training - Continuously evaluate, measure, and improve training effectiveness while implementing your action plan and adjust content or delivery methods to address any gaps or challenges faced by participants or yourself.

Adaptation and Flexibility - Remain open to feedback from trusted sources and be willing to adapt processes and methodologies based on evolving needs and circumstances.

Address Resistance - Proactively identify and address any resistance to the integration of A3 problem-solving, whether it stems from individuals or organizational culture. Encourage buy-in by highlighting success stories and demonstrating the tangible benefits of the approach if necessary.

Celebrate Successes - Recognize and celebrate successful problem-solving initiatives to reinforce their importance and encourage continued engagement and participation moving forward.

Advanced Techniques and Further Learning

For anyone looking to deepen their understanding of A3 problem-solving and take their improvement efforts to the next level, there are several advanced techniques and further learning resources available.

Advanced Problem-Solving Tools: To further advance your knowledge, you can explore advanced problem-solving tools and techniques such as *Six Sigma, Lean Six Sigma,* and *Design Thinking* to address complex and systemic issues. These methodologies offer additional frameworks and methodologies for problem-solving and process improvement.

Certification Programs: Organizations and individuals can pursue certification programs in A3 problem-solving, Lean Six Sigma, and other related disciplines to enhance their skills and credentials. These programs provide comprehensive training and certification in problem-solving methodologies and tools that can positively impact organizations and individuals alike.

Books and Publications: There are numerous valuable books, articles, and publications available on A3 problem-solving and other related topics more in depth. Organizations and individuals can leverage these resources to deepen their understanding of A3 problem-solving principles, learn from case studies and best practices, and stay informed about the latest developments in the field.

Here is a list of recommended books:

1. *"The Toyota Way to Lean Leadership: Achieving and Sustaining Excellence Through Leadership Development"* by Jeffrey K. Liker and Gary L. Convis - Explores Toyota's leadership principles and the role of A3 problem-solving in fostering a culture of continuous improvement.

2. *"The Toyota Way: 14 Management Principles from the World's Greatest Manufacturer"* by Jeffrey K. Liker - Offers insights into the principles and practices that underpin Toyota's renowned problem-solving culture, including the A3 problem-solving approach.

3. *"Managing to Learn: Using the A3 Management Process"* by John Shook - A practical guide to implementing the A3 management process, with examples and case studies from various industries.

4. *"Lean Thinking: Banish Waste and Create Wealth in Your Corporation"* by James P. Womack and Daniel T. Jones - Explores the principles of Lean thinking, including tools and techniques for process improvement and waste reduction, which complement A3 problem-solving.

5. *"Six Sigma: The Breakthrough Management Strategy Revolutionizing the World's Top Corporations"* by Mikel Harry and Richard Schroeder - Provides a comprehensive overview of the Six Sigma methodology, including DMAIC and statistical tools for process improvement.

6. *"Design Thinking: Integrating Innovation, Customer Experience, and Brand Value"* by Thomas Lockwood and Edgar Papke - Explores the principles of design thinking and its application in problem-solving, innovation, and customer-centric design.

7. *"Getting the Right Things Done: A Leader's Guide to Planning and Execution"* by Pascal Dennis - Provides a practical guide to implementing lean thinking and A3 problem-solving, with real-world examples and case studies.

By cultivating a culture of continuous improvement, integrating A3 problem-solving into daily operations, and exploring advanced techniques and further learning resources, you can embark on a journey of ongoing improvement and innovation, driving sustainable success, wisdom, as well as continuous growth.

Recap of Essential A3 Problem-Solving Concepts

Now that we've explored the fundamental principles of A3 problem-solving, let's recap some crucial concepts, topics, and definitions. These serve as your guiding factors for every problem-solving endeavor, ensuring consistent implementation and effectiveness. The A3 process will require various bouts of trial and error, which is why reviewing and polishing its steps continually is vital to producing powerful problem-solving procedures long-term.

Embrace these elements, refine them through practice, expand your knowledge on problem-solving, and build a robust foundation to tackle any challenge with confidence and success.

Key A3 Concepts

- **Understanding the Problem**: Thoroughly defining the problem and gathering data-driven insights is crucial for informed decision-making.
- **Root Cause Analysis**: Techniques like the 5 Whys and Fishbone Diagrams help identify underlying factors and drive sustainable solutions.
- **Developing Countermeasures**: Crafting viable solutions involves creativity, strategic thinking, and practical planning for implementation.
- **Continuous Improvement**: Integrating A3 problem-solving into daily operations fosters iterative learning and adaptation for ongoing enhancement.

- **Data-Driven Decision Making:** Relying on accurate data ensures effective problem-solving and increases the likelihood of success.
- **Reflection and Learning:** Embracing continuous learning and analyzing past experiences fosters a culture of improvement and innovation.

Key A3 Topics and Definitions

- **A3 Report:** A structured problem-solving approach that condenses complex issues onto a single A3-sized sheet of paper, facilitating concise communication and decision-making.

- **Root Cause Analysis:** A systematic process for identifying the underlying causes of problems or issues within an organization, aiming to address the fundamental factors contributing to undesirable outcomes.

- **5 Whys:** A technique for root cause analysis that involves repeatedly asking "why" to dig deeper into the underlying causes of a problem, typically reaching the root cause after five iterations.

- **Benchmarking:** The essential process of comparing one's practices, processes, or performance metrics to those of industry leaders and competitors to properly identify areas for improvement and best practices to emulate within your organization or situation

- **Pilot Program:** A small-scale implementation of a solution or initiative designed to test its feasibility, effectiveness, and impact before full-scale rollout.

- **Fishbone Diagram:** Also known as Ishikawa diagram or cause-and-effect diagram, it is a visual tool used to identify and organize potential causes of a problem, categorizing them into primary categories such as people, process, equipment, environment, and management.

Conclusion

As we conclude our journey through the intricacies of A3 problem-solving, let's pause to reflect on the valuable insights we've gained. Throughout our exploration, we've not only learned to decipher complex problems but also to unravel their underlying causes. We've honed our skills in crafting effective countermeasures and witnessed firsthand the transformative impact of data-driven decision-making. Additionally, we've come to appreciate the significance of fostering a culture of continuous improvement, where innovation thrives, and excellence becomes the norm.

It's essential to recognize that A3 is not merely a set of tools and techniques; it's a mindset—a way of approaching challenges with curiosity, creativity, and resilience. As we move forward in our problem-solving endeavors, let's embrace each obstacle as an opportunity for growth, recognizing that setbacks are valuable lessons in disguise. Let's celebrate our successes as milestones on the path to achieving our goals, knowing that our determination and perseverance will propel us forward.

So, as we bid farewell to this chapter of our journey, let's carry with us the lessons learned and the wisdom gained. Let's continue to question, innovate, and push the boundaries of what's possible. For our journey with A3 doesn't end here—it marks the beginning of a new chapter filled with endless possibilities and opportunities for growth.

www.ingramcontent.com/pod-product-compliance
Lightning Source LLC
Chambersburg PA
CBHW050324230526
45471CB00005B/2337